Walsingham

An Ever-Circling Year

Walsingham
An Ever-Circling Year

MARTIN WARNER

PHOTOGRAPHS BY PAUL BROWN AND KEN ADLARD

OXFORD UNIVERSITY PRESS
1996

Oxford University Press, Walton Street, Oxford OX2 6DP
Oxford New York
Athens Auckland Bangkok Bombay
Calcutta Cape Town Dar es Salaam Delhi
Florence Hong Kong Istanbul Karachi
Kuala Lumpur Madras Madrid Melbourne
Mexico City Nairobi Paris Singapore
Taipei Tokyo Toronto
and associated companies in
Berlin Ibadan

Oxford is a trade mark of Oxford University Press

British Library Cataloguing in Publication Data
Data available
ISBN 0–19–145690–X

10 9 8 7 6 5 4 3 2 1

Typeset in Adobe Minion
Printed in Hong Kong

For Nicholas, Elspeth, and Benjamin

FOREWORD

It may be that you are one of the quarter of a million pilgrims who visit Walsingham each year or perhaps your first acquaintance with 'England's Nazareth' will be through the pages of this book. The great humanist scholar Erasmus wrote after his pilgrimage that Walsingham was 'a town maintained by scarcely anything else but the number of its visitors'. Erasmus visited Walsingham in the sixteenth century, but as we approach the end of the present

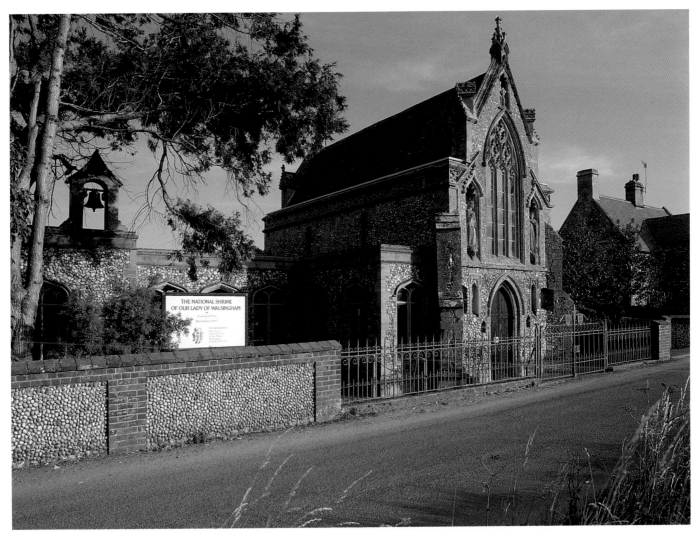

The Slipper Chapel

millennium the pilgrim hostels, shops, and chapels still testify to Walsingham's pre-eminence as a place of pilgrimage in England.

At the centre of any visit will be the two major Shrines of Our Lady of Walsingham. The Anglican Shrine is built around the Holy House—a replica of the house at Nazareth in which Mary received the gracious invitation of our God that she would become the Mother of his Son. There is a stillness in the Holy House that speaks to pilgrims of the peace given to Mary that allowed her to respond, 'Let it be to me as you have said.' In Saint Luke's gospel we hear of Mary's anxiety and her struggle to understand the events involving her; we also hear of the grace moving her to greater faith, hope, and love for God and his great plan of salvation.

A walk along the 'Holy Mile' to Houghton St Giles brings you to the fourteenth-century Slipper Chapel, which is the National Shrine of England's Roman Catholics. This was the last chapel in which many medieval pilgrims lingered before entering the holy ground of Walsingham. Younger

pilgrims still remove footwear at the Slipper Chapel as they enter the domain of Walsingham and its Shrines. Over 900 years may separate us from our companions of earlier times, but the same weariness and common burdens still mark the lives of all women and men in this difficult world.

The gifts of Walsingham are many. The 'Walsingham Ballad' published in the reign of Henry VII speaks of innumerable miracles, of grace 'dayly shewed to men of every age'; 'Lame made hole and blynde restored to syghte'. I am sometimes asked if there are still miracles in Walsingham. There are sometimes particular instances of God's healing touch recorded, but perhaps more important is that pilgrims to this holy place still find a renewed peace, a wholeness, and a vision that gives them courage to return home refreshed and with a determination one day to return to Walsingham.

Father Martin's text and Ken Adlard and Paul Brown's illustrations show us something of the rich variety of Walsingham. Medieval history and the twentieth century mingle easily here as close neighbours. Sadly the original Shrine and Holy House were destroyed in 1538. Nearly 250 years afterwards the servant of God's Word, John Wesley, preached at Walsingham: 'I walked over what is left of the famous Abbey . . . had there been a grain of virtue or public spirit in Henry the Eighth, these noble buildings need not have run to ruin.'

In these happier times pilgrims can explore the Orthodox Chapel of Saint Seraphim established in 1967 at the old village railway station with its icons that speak so powerfully of heaven. The Georgian Methodist Chapel, the oldest still in use in East Anglia, provides a haven on busy pilgrimage days. The chapels and gardens of the Anglican and Roman Catholic Shrines have a place for every visitor and every need.

The Anglican Shrine

What is required of the modern pilgrim-visitor to Walsingham? The rich mix of people evident on bank holidays and during large pilgrimages warns against an easy answer. Walsingham is for peoples of all faiths and none. We welcome old and young, strangers and friends. We simply invite you to join us. At the heart of our faith is that an encounter with our God can be a very personal and unique event; it was in the holy house of Nazareth that Mary was given her special mission and grace.

This book will give an impression of Walsingham and will point us to its mystery. It still remains for pilgrim-visitors to discover the significance of Walsingham for themselves. For some the visit to the Slipper Chapel or Holy House will be of greatest significance; for others there will be a unique sacred place waiting for them in the holy land of Walsingham.

The Anglican and Roman Catholic Shrines remain committed to close collaboration in a spirit of trust and mutual learning. Increasing numbers of visitors are now members of ecumenical pilgrimages. The Holy Mile is common to all pilgrims just as the sprinkling at the Holy Well each afternoon is a means of God's grace regardless of Christian denomination.

During the pilgrim year joint events and services are organized by the two Shrines. Each August the Feast of the Assumption is celebrated by a common walk of witness and prayer between the Anglican and Roman Catholic parish churches ending in the grounds of the Anglican Shrine with festivities and fireworks.

There is all too easily mistrust between divided Christians. It would be misguided and naïve to suggest that in Walsingham we are immune from that difficult aspect of our Christian heritage. Yet over the years in Walsingham there has been a commitment to a common search for God's word to us and a readiness like Mary to listen and where possible to act. Above all there is a shared determination to take seriously the challenge of the gospel—

'May they all be one,
just as, Father, you are in me and I am in you,
so that they also may be in us,
so that the world may believe it was you who sent me.'

JOHN 17: 21

The Christian community of Walsingham and all our friends of goodwill welcome you to England's Nazareth. We share a common mission and Father Martin's book is one expression of that vision. Yet in Walsingham we have no sense of a burden or heavy responsibility for the success or otherwise of your pilgrimage to this holy place. Sacred places do their work regardless of the efforts of local villagers and Shrine Administrators. The end point of every successful pilgrimage to Walsingham is the open heart of an individual before God. Mary's silent encounter with the living God in the heart of the holy house of Nazareth is a story for all times and peoples, a story at the very heart of Walsingham. May God bless all of us who read and use this book.

THE REVEREND ALAN WILLIAMS, SM
Director of the Roman Catholic National Shrine of Our Lady

CONTENTS

ACKNOWLEDGEMENTS

The author and publishers wish to record their gratitude to everybody who has contributed to the making of this book. Thanks are due in particular to the staff at the Roman Catholic and Anglican Shrines, for their co-operation during the taking of many photographs; to the Walsingham Estate Company for permission to take photographs within the Abbey grounds; and to many pilgrims and visitors for their interest in and forbearance with any disruptions caused during photography.

Excerpts from the New Jerusalem Bible, (pp. 3, 7, 11, 12, 15, 16, 19, 25, 31, 33, 34, 37, 41, 42, 47, 51, 55, 56, 60, 63, 66, 70, 73, 76, 77, 83, 85) published and copyright 1985 by Darton, Longman, and Todd Ltd. and Doubleday & Co Inc., and used by permission of the publishers.

Prayers from The Divine Office (pp. 6, 10, 14, 18, 29, 44, 50, 54, 58) published in *Morning and Evening Prayer* (HarperCollins), altered with permission. Reproduced by permission of A. P. Watt Ltd. on behalf of The Hierarchies of England & Wales, Ireland, and Australia.

Excerpts from the English translation of *The Roman Missal* © 1973, International Committee on English in the Liturgy, Inc. (ICEL); excerpts from the English translation of *Holy Communion and Worship of the Eucharist outside Mass* © 1974, ICEL. All rights reserved; altered with permission. Reproduced by permission of the International Commission on English in the Liturgy.

Prayer (p. 40) from *The Alternative Service Book 1980.* Copyright © The Central Board of Finance of the Church of England. Used with permission.

INTRODUCTION

Walsingham is about vision. It began with the vision of Richeldis in 1061 in which she was shown Mary's house in Nazareth and was inspired to build a replica here in England. That house, destroyed in the Reformation and restored by Anglicans in 1931, focuses our attention on Mary's vision; her perception of her vocation to be the mother of Jesus and her understanding of the graciousness of God, expressed in her song, the Magnificat. Perhaps most profoundly and simply, however, Walsingham is about a vision of Jesus, seen here as the child of Mary, the Word made flesh, in whom we find healing, joy, and peace.

Many thousands of pilgrims come to Walsingham each year in search of the presence of God, bringing the recognition of

Common Place

a need for healing. Following in the footsteps of medieval pilgrims they pass through the village of Houghton St Giles, in which is situated the beautiful fourteenth-century Slipper Chapel. It was here that pilgrims removed their shoes to walk the last mile barefoot, a sign of penitence. This is now the site of the Roman Catholic National Shrine of Our Lady of Walsingham and is dominated by the modern Chapel of Reconciliation, a powerful reminder of the unity into which Jesus calls his disciples in order that the world might believe.

This book is offered as an account of the vision of Walsingham. The photographs by Paul Brown and Ken Adlard skilfully capture the atmosphere of this strangely holy place, and in so doing evoke the story and significance of Mary's child. His story is not confined simply to Pales-

tine under Roman occupation two thousand years ago, however. Each year it unfolds in the life of the Church as the seasons proclaim a movement from death to new life, providing within the order of creation a drama and symbol for the interpretation of the Christian faith.

The division of the book into four sections allows each season to be used as a dramatic stage on which some particular aspect of the Walsingham vision is to be seen. Three of these are associated with the form of prayer which uses a rosary to meditate on the birth, death, and resurrection of Jesus.

Winter conjures up images of Christmas and is used here as the backdrop to the cycle of joyful events surrounding the birth of Jesus.

The Chapel of Reconciliation

The preparation of the earth for planting and the sowing of seed in dark furrows are the signs of spring and the anticipation of new life. This is the season within which the sorrowful narrative of the death of Jesus is told.

Summer harvest is used in the New Testament as a symbol of the resurrection; Jesus is described as the first fruits and the theme of gathering together the whole crop is symbolic of the creation which is in the process of fulfilling its perfect destiny. This is the season in which the glorious accounts of the significance of the resurrection are told.

Autumn is that mellow season in which we look forward to new beginnings, the starting of a new academic year. We reflect too on the passing of time, in falling summer leaves and darker nights, and November remembrances call to mind our dead; some loved, some respected, some just a name, but all alike reminding us that death is part of human life, and for Christians the beginning of our life in baptism, sharing in the death of Jesus, in order that we might also share in his resurrection. Against this backdrop have been placed the Baptismal Mysteries—aspects of the Christian life. These too can form a part of the circle of meditations using the rosary.

For many Christians the rosary is a form of meditation by which the mind and body are drawn into a rhythm of prayer so that the imagination can be set free to absorb a particular story or mystery in the life of Jesus. Each bead, the chain, and the cross which together form a rosary are used for saying a particular prayer as they are counted off between finger and thumb, employing the hands in a manner intended to still the distractions of the body. On the cross is said the Apostles' Creed; on the first single bead and by way of introduction the Lord's Prayer; three Hail Marys on the next three beads; and the Glory Be on the chain which leads to the beginning of the next cycle on a single bead.

The rest of the rosary is divided into five groups of ten beads, each group preceded by a single bead. The sequences of joyful, sorrowful, glorious, and in this book baptismal mysteries all have five episodes, a set of ten beads plus a single one for each. As with the introduction, the Lord's Prayer is said on the single bead, Hail Mary on each of the ten beads which follow, and Glory Be on the chain which leads to the next single bead.

You may have bought this book simply as a pictorial record of Walsingham; if so, I hope that its stories will remind you of the vision which animates the life of this pilgrimage centre. You may find that the structure of the rosary is quite incidental to your interest; perhaps the circle of the seasons of the year depicted here will lead you deeper into an understanding of the mystery of the passing of time and of the incarnation celebrated in human history through the lives of the baptized. But you may wish to use these stories, the words of scripture, and pictures of England's Nazareth to pray the rosary, perhaps something you have never done before. Whatever your choice, may the movement of the Holy Spirit upon your imagination enable you to experience through an ever-circling year the vision of Walsingham in which, with Mary, you gaze upon the glory of God revealed in the face of Jesus Christ.

WINTER
Joyful
Mysteries

GABRIEL'S MESSAGE

Walsingham is set in lush and fertile countryside. Everything teems with life. This is rich farmland, growing corn, wheat and barley, fruit and vegetables, and with good grazing for livestock. The farms here have sometimes been in the same family for generations, reflecting stability and order.

God said, 'Let the earth produce vegetation: seed-bearing plants, and fruit trees on earth, bearing fruit with their seed inside, each corresponding to its own species.' And so it was.

God said, 'Let there be lights in the vault of heaven to divide day from night, and let them indicate festivals, days and years. Let them be lights in the vault of heaven to shine on the earth.' And so it was.

God said, 'Let the waters be alive with a swarm of living creatures, and let birds wing their way above the earth across the vault of heaven.' And so it was.

God said, 'Let the earth produce every kind of living creature in its own species: cattle, creeping things and wild animals of all kinds.' And so it was.

God said, 'Let us make man in our own image, in the likeness of ourselves.'

> God created man in the image of himself,
> in the image of God he created him,
> male and female he created them.

And so it was. God saw all he had made, and indeed it was very good.

The Walsingham year begins here, with the story of creation and its mirror image, the story of redemption. It begins with the message from God of a whole new life. Deep in winter, preparations for Christmas take us back to the memory of Gabriel's message, and in particular, the opening words, 'Rejoice, you who enjoy God's favour! The Lord is with you.' Joy and hope are God's gifts to his people in a cold and darkened world.

But the arrival of the message has a startling quality about it. 'Look, I am doing something new, now it emerges; can you not see it?' The whole of human history has led to this moment and provided the signs, symbols, and language by which it can be understood. From within creation God takes to himself the means by which all time, all peoples, everything that exists can be restored and perfected.

The Abbey Grounds

For this monumental task God asks in simplicity for the co-operation of one woman and one man, each to respond in a different way, offering that of which they are capable, that which their love makes possible. Mary, you are to conceive and bear a son, and you must name him Jesus. Joseph, take Mary home as your wife. She has conceived what is in her by the Holy Spirit; her son is the one who is to save his people from their sins.

In the Anglican Shrine

Lord, open our hearts to your grace.
Through the angel's message to Mary
we have learned to believe
in the incarnation of Christ your Son.
Lead us by his passion and cross
to the glory of the resurrection.
We make this prayer through our Lord. Amen.

MARY'S PILGRIMAGE

Good news, really good news, does have a strange effect on us. It's never quite complete unless there has been someone to share it with. Perhaps it's the person you love most, perhaps it's an almost complete stranger, perhaps it's the whole world, but you have to tell someone. Good news is made for sharing. It's a gift which brings laughter and celebration to others.

How beautiful on the mountains,
are the feet of the messenger
   announcing peace,
of the messenger of good news,
who proclaims salvation
and says to Zion,
'Your God is king!'
The voices of your watchmen!
Now they raise their voices,
shouting for joy together,
for with their own eyes they have
   seen
Yahweh returning to Zion.
Break into shouts together,
shouts of joy, you ruins of Jerusalem;
for Yahweh has consoled his people,
he has redeemed Jerusalem.
Yahweh has bared his holy arm
for all the nations to see,
and all the ends of the earth
have seen the salvation of our God.

ISAIAH 52: 7–10

To share her joy, Mary sets out to visit her cousin Elizabeth. The news she carries breaks out in a cascade of happy song which expresses the hope they know God has planted in their hearts. These two women are sisters in liberation, for in themselves they carry the vindication of their longing.

The song Mary sings sets the tone of the atmosphere of the dawn of salvation. For God 'has pulled down princes from their thrones and raised high the lowly. He has filled the starving with good things, sent the rich away empty.' And in recognition of all this the child stirs in Elizabeth's womb; a mysterious statement of inarticulate faith, characteristic of those who wait for liberation and the dawning light of the kingdom of God.

But amid all this rejoicing there is a sombre note. Travel is not always easy. It can be a lonely and painful road that leads to the downtrodden and oppressed who wait to hear the good news of freedom. Mary embarks on that journey as a woman of courage and compassion. She is an evangelist who makes her way to those from whom there will be a stirring of response, as there was in Elizabeth.

Mary journeys like a prophetic figure of the past to the 'ruins of Jerusalem', which represent the wastelands of any city, to those who live in the dust of the streets, to the exile, and to the refugee. She carries the child of her womb in order to bring hope and new life. Softly she knocks at a door; it opens, and inside we find the hungry and the thirsty, the stranger and those without clothing, the sick, and people in prison. And the child stirs within her.

The Holy House

PRAYER

Almighty, ever-living God,
you inspired the Blessed Virgin Mary,
when she was carrying your Son,
to visit Elizabeth.
Grant that, always docile to the voice of the
    Spirit,
we may, together with our Lady, glorify your
    name.
We make this prayer through our Lord. Amen.

THE NATIVITY

Arise, shine out, for your light has come,
and the glory of Yahweh has risen on you.
Look! though night still covers the earth
and darkness the peoples,
on you Yahweh is rising
and over you his glory can be seen.
The nations will come to your light
and kings to your dawning brightness.
Lift up your eyes and look around:
all are assembling and coming towards you,
your sons coming from far away
and your daughters being carried on the hip.

Your oppressors' children will humbly
    approach you,
at your feet all who despised you will fall.

ISAIAH 60: 1–4, 14

From the Chapel of Reconciliation

There is a story that, at the time of the birth of Jesus, the message of the angels was also witnessed by a young Roman soldier who was returning to Bethlehem to work on the census. He was strangely and powerfully moved by the angels' song, and followed the shepherds in the direction of the town.

The soldier abandoned his horse, which seemed no longer suitable for this journey and, as they approached the lights of the town, he exchanged his military cloak for that of a peasant, beneath which his armour could be disguised. He followed the shepherds to the stable and, captivated by the simplicity of this miracle of new life, knelt and gazed with pure joy at the sight of the tiny child.

His attention was momentarily distracted by the child's mother, who shivered in a cold draught. Without thought or hesitation he took off his cloak and offered it to Joseph for his wife. Instantly the shepherds recoiled from the soldier, his breastplate now gleaming in the light and revealing clearly an embossed figure of the she-wolf suckling the twin founders of an empire which already tyrannized more than half the known world, and of which he was the potent symbol. The soldier swiftly drew his sword and turned. 'Take note', he said to the shepherds, 'of what you have seen, and say nothing.' With these words he slid the sword into the hay beneath the manger and went out, back into the night.

Joseph covered his head, murmuring softly a scripture from the prophet Isaiah: 'The wolf will live with the lamb, the panther lie down with the kid, calf, lion and fat-stock beast together, with a little boy to lead them.' 'It will happen in the final days', continued Mary, 'that they will hammer their swords into ploughshares and their spears into sickles. Nation will not lift sword against nation, no longer will they learn how to make war.' 'House of Jacob, come, let us walk in the Lord's light', concluded Joseph, 'for today in your sight these scriptures are being fulfilled.'

That young soldier appeared again, just over thirty years later, in the pages of the gospel, when he put into simple and eloquent words the great truth he had witnessed in the Bethlehem stable.

13

PRAYER

By the long-awaited coming of your
  new-born Son
deliver us, Lord,
from the age-old bondage of sin.
We make our prayer through our Lord. Amen.

THE BRIGHTNESS OF HIS GLORY

There was something about her which you couldn't quite define. In her smile, a quality of lambent radiance, laughter in her eyes, but sadness too, and at certain times she seemed absorbed in a different realm, more real to her than the world we live in. But mainly it was in her eyes. That's where you could tell that she had seen, in the fraction of a moment when the veil had been lifted aside, the glory of heaven, and nothing on earth would ever be quite the same again.

He sat down opposite the treasury and watched the people putting money into the treasury, and many of the rich put in a great deal. A poor widow came and put in two small coins, the equivalent of a penny. Then he called his disciples and said to them, 'In truth I tell you, this poor widow has put more in than all who have contributed to the treasury; for they have all put in money they could spare, but she in her poverty has put in everything she possessed, all she had to live on.'

MARK 12: 41–4   15

Some things in the Temple hadn't changed. For the faithful old women who loved and served God it had always been a kind of home. And it was one of them who had recognized Jesus when he was first brought to the Temple as a babe in his parents' arms: Anna, the daughter of Phanuel, who was 84 years old. What a strange person she was, and how odd her life had been. Perhaps it was the sadness of a brief and inconclusive marriage which haunted her appearance and behaviour. And yet, there was something radiant, something in her eyes which caught the brightness of the glory of God.

She had caught that brightness in the face of the child Jesus. Some impulse had prompted her to make her way through the Temple at that particular moment, and from a lifetime's habit of reflecting upon the presence of God she had recognized and seen him there, in an unlikely bundle of blankets and baby clothes. That simple moment of recognition was the profoundest encounter of her life. It made sense of everything that she had done and been; it made her an evangelist. 'She spoke of the child to all who looked forward to the deliverance of Jerusalem.'

Anna is one of a great army of evangelists who witness to the presence of God in a particular way. Go into any church which has that unmistakable atmosphere of prayer, and there will be someone like Anna who potters in to do what needs doing, who will light candles, rattle through a decade of the rosary, mutter her way through the Stations of the Cross, and with unselfconscious regularity present herself at the communion rail and in the confessional. For her all of this will seem quite normal, and rarely will she think to comment upon it in any way that is different from her comments on the tragedy of a recent disaster, or news of one of the grandchildren.

But when the thin steel of cynical secularism slices into the intricate tapestry of the Church's faith, and when the Church herself seems bent on self-destruction and denial, Anna, with her army of evangelists, will continue to point to the reality of the presence of God, revealed to any who in love and simplicity have stooped to see. Yes, there is something in her eyes which has caught the brightness of the glory of God.

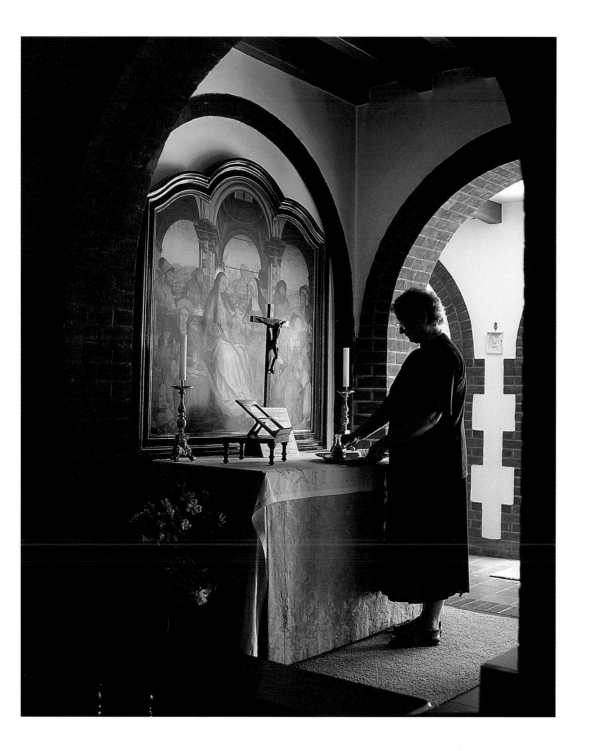

PRAYER

Almighty, ever-living God,
your Only-begotten Son
was presented in the temple,
in flesh and blood like ours:
purify us in mind and heart
that we may meet you in your
*   glory.*
We make this prayer through
*   our Lord. Amen*

TO BE FOUND IN THE TEMPLE

One of the things that everyone remembered about him was the way he asked questions. They had a kind of directness which made you think before you answered, and yet at the same time they invited trust and honesty. Perhaps you never remembered that there was little small talk, since he was never difficult to be with.

How I love your Law!
I ponder it all day long.
You make me wiser than my enemies
by your commandment which is
    mine for ever.
I am wiser than all my teachers
because I ponder your instructions.
I have more understanding than the
    aged
because I keep your precepts.
I restrain my foot from evil paths
to keep your word.
I do not turn aside from your
    judgements,
because you yourself have instructed
    me.
How pleasant your promise to my
    palate,
sweeter than honey in my mouth!
From your precepts I learn wisdom,
so I hate all deceptive ways.

PSALM 119: 97–104   19

Even at the age of twelve a young lad is vulnerable on his own in a big city. It would have been natural for his parents to worry. But the one thing which had captivated him was the chance to ask those questions he had always wanted to put to the Temple theologians: what is the connection between healing and forgiveness? Is it permitted on the Sabbath day to save life, or to kill? Who is the greatest among us? Which is the first commandment? Teach me to pray.

Questions like these are generally tied up with our own experiences, emerging from those points in our life when a theoretical situation becomes my situation. Should I have an abortion? Did I sack her because she is black, or because she's a woman and has got a degree (which I haven't), and an answer for everything? Could I have avoided that pram if I'd said no to another pint? But we love each other, is it so wrong? I wonder if he overheard what I said?

The most tragic response to questions like these is something along the lines of 'so what? . . . who cares? . . . it's none of your business anyway'. But actually if parents, or friends, or partners care, it is their business. Jesus opens up the questioning of the law in the context of God's relationship as a loving parent with the entire human family. These are the matters which are closest to his Father's heart, the issues and the means by which human beings become fully alive and reveal the glory of their creating. For a moment all of this has distracted his attention and taken Jesus away from his immediate family; eventually it will consume his whole life.

What should I do? What do I want? Would it be right? These questions still distract us from the everyday routine. When we take the crossroads of our lives to the teachers of the faith, we should expect them to direct us to Jesus who asks us to take for granted the parent's love which says: 'I care, you are not alone; your actions belong to the history of all humanity, engraved upon my hands.'

Father in heaven, creator of all,
you ordered the earth to bring forth life
and crowned its goodness by creating
  the human family.
In history's moment when all was ready,
you sent your Son to dwell in time,
obedient to the laws of life in our world.

Teach us the sanctity of human love,
show us the value of family life,
and help us to live in peace with all men
  and women
that we may share in your life for ever.
  Amen.

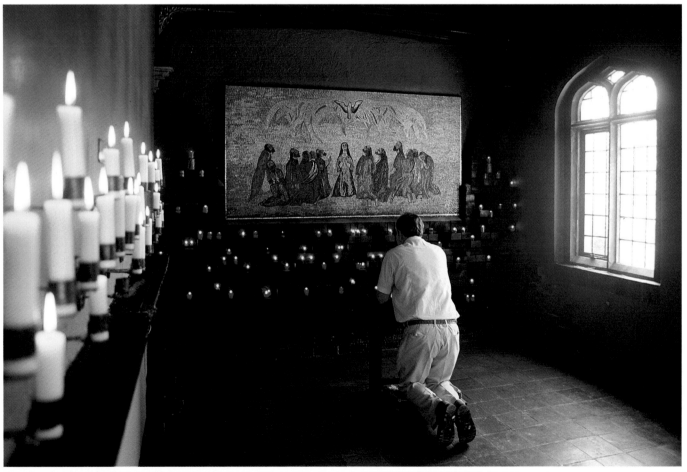

The Chapel of the Holy Ghost

SPRING

Sorrowful Mysteries

THE STRUGGLE WITHIN

There are two moments in the gospels when we are given a glimpse of Jesus' innermost struggle with his vocation. The first is in the story of the temptations in the wilderness and the second is in the account of his agony in the garden of Gethsemane.

In some ways they are very similar experiences. The intimidating darkness of the night when he is arrested is reminiscent of the bleak desolation of the wilderness. The wild animals of the desert are now matched by the menacing patrol of the Temple Guard. Against this bewildering backdrop Jesus confronts the agony of an inescapable situation. This is the moment of abandonment to the will of God, his own vocation.

For me, Yahweh's word has been the cause
of insult and derision all day long.
I would say to myself, 'I will not think about him,
I will not speak in his name any more,'
but then there seemed to be a fire burning in my heart,
imprisoned in my bones.
The effort to restrain it wearied me,
I could not do it.
I heard so many disparaging me,
'Terror on every side!
Denounce him! Let us denounce him!'

Yahweh Sabaoth, you who test the upright,
observer of motives and thoughts, I shall see your
vengeance on them,
for I have revealed my cause to you.
Sing to Yahweh,
praise Yahweh,
for he has delivered the soul of one in need
from the clutches of evil doers.

JEREMIAH 20: 8–10, 12–13   25

Jesus experiences the mystery of suffering, that darkness for which there can be no explanation or adequate reason, only faith and hope and love. This is the moment of those who wait at the roadside with the victims of a fatal accident, at the bedside of a person who has Aids. This is the prison cell of people who have mysteriously disappeared, the inescapable memories of childhood abuse, the deep but invisible wounds of an unwanted divorce, or the silent ache of bereavement.

But there is always hope. The mystery of this suffering is also the pain and struggle of childbirth. We are confronted by the nature of our human condition. That which is stored up inside us must find new expression. In the sign of the tearing of flesh God's work of reconciliation is accomplished, and angels wait to minister. An echo is heard from the past; Mary pants and gasps for air, crying out in giving birth to the fulfilment of the longing of the prophet, 'I shall lead the blind by a road they do not know, by paths they do not know I shall conduct them. I shall turn the darkness into light before them.'

Sunrise at Wells

PRAYER

Father in heaven,
the light of your truth bestows
sight
to the darkness of sinful eyes.
May the repentance of our sins
bring us the blessing of your
forgiveness
and the gift of your light.
We ask this in the name of
Jesus, the Lord. Amen.

Sunset by the
Chapel of Reconciliation

THEY PLOUGHED MY BACK

Scourging is all part of the process; it's the way they carry out the death penalty. This small detail in the description of the process of law connects Jesus with a barbaric system of punishment all too well attested by writers outside the Christian tradition. Martin Hegel has surveyed the evidence, and comments that although the form of execution could vary enormously, normally 'it included a flogging beforehand, and the victim often carried the beam to the place of execution, where he was nailed to it with outstretched arms, raised up and seated on a small wooden peg.'

'They have pressed me hard from my youth,'
this is Israel's song,
'They have pressed me hard from my youth
but could never destroy me.

They ploughed my back like ploughmen,
drawing long furrows.
But the Lord who is just, has destroyed
the yoke of the wicked.'

The Slipper Chapel

This episode in the Lord's passion brings us face to face with reality. The Romans really did this kind of thing. The passion was not only mental anguish; it cut into the flesh and made him bleed. Jesus was bound to our human nature with as much reality as he was bound to the pillar and scourged.

In an ancient homily for Holy Saturday Jesus cries out to Adam and the entire human race, 'See the scourging of my back, which I accepted in order to disperse the load of your sins which was laid upon your back.' Our lives are now intertwined with his life, our suffering, fear, hurt, and sin being taken into his body and redeemed.

Ploughed fields are a particular feature of the landscape in spring. The earth is turned and broken, passive in the expectation of crops and the harvest. This is an image evoked in the New Testament: 'Now be patient, brothers, until the Lord's coming. Think of a farmer: how patiently he waits for the precious fruit of the ground.' 'Think of our Lord's patience as your opportunity to be saved.'

The ploughed furrows in the bare earth of spring fields remind us of our origin and our destiny. We were taken from the earth, made by God in his image and the breath of life breathed into us by him. In death we are returned to the earth. But the earth can also be for us an image of Jesus, the patient (which also means suffering) Jesus, the furrows of human sins ploughed upon his back. In him, 'What is sown is perishable, but what is raised is imperishable; what is sown is contemptible but what is raised is glorious'.

Lord,
by the suffering of Christ your Son
you have saved us all from the death
we inherited from sinful Adam,
whose sinful likeness,
by the law of nature, we have borne.

May the sanctifying power of grace
help us to put on the likeness of our Lord
in heaven,
who lives and reigns for ever and ever.
Amen.

THE CROWN OF THORNS

So many of the things that Jesus said and did turn the value systems of the world upside-down: 'anyone who wants to be first among you must be slave to all.' This theme in his teaching manifests itself in the events of his passion. He enters Jerusalem acclaimed as a king, yet riding on a donkey. The disciples' master is also their servant, a suffering servant who gives them an example to follow.

Here is my servant whom I uphold,
my chosen one in whom my soul
    delights.
I have sent my spirit upon him,
he will bring fair judgement to the
    nations.
He does not cry out or raise his voice,
his voice is not heard in the street;
he does not break the crushed reed
or snuff the faltering wick.

I, Yahweh, have called you in saving
    justice,
I have grasped you by the hand and
    shaped you;
I have made you a covenant of the
    people
and light to the nations,
to open the eyes of the blind,
to free captives from prison,
and those who live in darkness from
    the dungeon.

ISAIAH 42: 1–3, 6–7   33

Within the Slipper Chapel

It is often small things that trigger the great moments of our lives. A casual word plants the germ of an idea for a chosen career or profession. A chance meeting might lead to getting to know the person you eventually marry. Among the many words and phrases from his youth which resonated in his memory, might not Jesus have been influenced by the echo of a familiar song, 'He hath put down the mighty from their seat: and hath exalted the humble and meek'?

The crown of thorns does not confer sovereignty and the dignity of state, but signifies the exaltation of the person who brings liberation and hope to those who live by the values of the gospel. In this coronation Jesus vindicates the blessedness of those who are persecuted in the cause of right, those who hunger and thirst for justice, and all who are peacemakers. He is gentle, poor in spirit, merciful and pure of heart, and the world laughs.

Mockery and distortion are perhaps the cruellest and most abiding terrors of this episode. It is they which are most destructive of genuine innocence, filling the imagination with hideous parody. Another three Kings approach the Christ child, bearing gifts in luxuriant wrappings. Their fawning smiles are the thin veneer of treachery and when they have gone their presents yield a blindfold, a length of purple cloth, and a pair of secateurs.

'Blessed are you when people abuse you and persecute you and speak all kinds of calumny against you falsely on my account. Rejoice and be glad, for your reward will be great in heaven; this is how they persecuted the prophets before you.' The crown of your blessedness is that worn by Jesus himself.

35

The Anglican Shrine grounds

PRAYER

Father all-powerful, God of love,
you have raised our Lord Jesus Christ from
    death to life,
resplendent in glory as King of creation.

Open our hearts,
free all the world to rejoice in his peace,
to glory in his justice, to live in his love.
Bring all humanity together in Jesus Christ your
    Son,
whose kingdom is with you and the Holy Spirit,
one God, for ever and ever. Amen.

CARRYING THE CROSS

Student Cross Pilgrimage

On ashtrays and bookmarks, t-shirts and coffee mugs, you will find that comment which so eloquently expresses a ubiquitous facet of life today, especially when behind the wheel of a car: 'O Lord, make me patient, but hurry!'

Anyone who has ever been on a pilgrimage will know, however, that speed is not always possible or desirable. Perhaps the most obvious example of this is the great procession which is characteristic of most pilgrimage centres. The procession takes time to form: we have to wait for those in front to move off, and sometimes allow those behind us to catch up. At the head of us goes the cross; we are a pilgrim people who carry the cross.

He called the people and his disciples to him and said, 'If anyone wants to be a follower of mine, let him renounce himself and take up his cross and follow me. Anyone who wants to save his life will lose it; but anyone who loses his life for my sake, and for the sake of the gospel, will save it. What gain, then, is it for anyone to win the whole world and forfeit his life? . . . For if anyone in this sinful and adulterous generation is ashamed of me and of my words, the Son of man will also be ashamed of him when he comes in the glory of his Father with the holy angels.'

MARK 8: 34–8   37

Neither in its original context, nor in our understanding of this duty today, does the carrying of the cross seem to be something that we can hurry. For each individual, it is a vocation for life, sometimes chosen, sometimes given apparently without much choice. A lone parent with three young children may have had little or no choice over the circumstances which created that situation. Many people struggle to remain faithful to their vocation, through marriage vows, religious vows, ordination vows, etc. They know that these can be both a joyful experience and a painful cross, the implications of which often have to be worked out afresh in the changing contexts of life.

Sometimes we cannot know what, for certain people—special people—the carrying of the cross is like. In the mysterious world of mental illness the cross may be all too clearly known, but unexplained in terms which are easily understood. In the lives of those who are severely handicapped the cross emerges with particular clarity, calling us to see the healing and redemptive love of God at work in ways which may not always satisfy the narrow definitions of our achievement-orientated culture.

It would, of course, be possible to extend the list of those who carry a special cross and understand its mystery in hidden ways. Perhaps the significance of this is not only in what they perceive, but also in how we respond to them. With absolute clarity Jesus asks us never to be ashamed of a person who carries the cross. Perhaps it is that which makes our processions so special and so different from the ways of the world. As pilgrims, we wait upon those who carry a special cross. Perhaps they are slower, more difficult to understand, and very demanding of our love and patience. Embracing them brings us to Jesus and the foot of his cross. There we meet Mary, who is not ashamed to be his mother, encouraging us not to be ashamed to be their brothers and sisters.

PRAYER *Almighty Father,*
look with mercy on this your family
for which our Lord Jesus Christ
  was content to be betrayed
  and given up into the hands of wicked men
  and to suffer death upon the cross;
who is alive and glorified
  with you and the Holy Spirit
one God, now and for ever. Amen.

The Anglican
National Pilgrimage

DEATH ON THE CROSS

The eyes have been closed for some time, the breathing difficult and laboured. It stops for the last time. He is dead. It is finished.

Often the surroundings in which we die are orderly and controlled. In the hospital or hospice, even at home with nursing care, we prepare for death. There may be time to reflect, time to pray, time to ask others to pray with us, calling a priest to celebrate in word and sacrament the culmination of baptismal life for one of God's children.

'Now the hour has come
for the Son of man to be glorified.
In all truth I tell you,
unless a wheat grain falls into the earth and dies,
it remains only a single grain;
but if it dies
it yields a rich harvest.
Anyone who loves his life loses it;
anyone who hates his life in this world
will keep it for eternal life.
Whoever serves me, must follow me,
and my servant will be with me wherever I am.
If anyone serves me, my Father will honour him.
Now my soul is troubled.
What shall I say:
Father, save me from this hour?
But it is for this very reason that I have come to this hour.
Father, glorify your name!'

JOHN 12: 23–8

St Mary's graveyard

41

Spring brings round the time to turn again to the dark furrows of the earth and sow seed for the harvest. It is a story as old as humanity itself, as familiar as life and death. And although nothing can ever adequately express the gnawing sense of loss which we call bereavement, yet to liken this to the sowing of seed is to affirm that there is always hope and new life and joy in the harvest: 'Those who sow in tears sing as they reap.'

But this is not the whole story. The human experience of death does not neatly coincide with the orderly passing of the seasons, and from even the most tranquil of deathbeds there comes the cry of defiance which proclaims that this is not the way God intended life to be. Death is the expression of brokenness and incompletion. It reminds us that the world is also unjust and we are capable of terrible crimes.

Our impression that this is so is confirmed by the woman who stands at the foot of the cross. Calmly, she speaks: 'His life was begun beneath the shadow of tyranny and exile, amid massacre and bloodshed. Now the blood of every innocent victim of violence, injustice, and cruelty runs from his head and hands and side. But of this moment the prophet has spoken and said, "Thus says Yahweh, the redeemer, the Holy One of Israel, to the one who is despised, detested by the nation, to the slave of despots: 'Kings will stand up when they see, princes will see and bow low, because of Yahweh who is faithful, the Holy One of Israel who has chosen you.'"'

The body laid in the hollow of the earth is the sign of vindication and joy at the time of the harvest.

PRAYER

Almighty, ever-living God,
whose Only-begotten Son
*   descended to the realm of the*
*   dead,*
and rose from there to glory,
grant that your faithful people,
who were buried with him in
*   baptism,*
may, by his resurrection,
*   obtain eternal life.*
We make our prayer through
*   our Lord. Amen.*

SUMMER
Glorious Mysteries

WITNESSING THE RESURRECTION

The question they all asked was, 'Who is she?' When the accounts were written and circulated, she was the person who featured most prominently. Some people knew her, however, and some did not approve. The things that he had said and done were generally praiseworthy; but to consort with women of this kind was surely asking for trouble. How wrong they were.

From now onwards, then, we will not consider anyone by human standards: even if we were once familiar with Christ according to human standards, we do not know him in that way any longer. So for anyone who is in Christ, there is a new creation: the old order is gone and a new being is there to see. It is all God's work; he reconciled us to himself through Christ and he gave us the ministry of reconciliation. I mean, God was in Christ reconciling the world to himself, not holding anyone's faults against them, but entrusting to us the message of reconciliation.

2 CORINTHIANS 5: 16–19   47

Luke is the only evangelist who makes any reference to Mary Magdalene, other than noting her presence at the tomb; she was the woman from whom seven demons had been cast out. Something had changed fundamentally in her life when she encountered Jesus, and from that moment she had become a new creation.

But traces of the old life must have haunted her still. Around Jerusalem she passed familiar street corners, the houses of those she had known before, the bazaar where she had been a predictable figure, and forbidden sites, where religious people did not want to be reminded of her presence. Now, as she made her way to the tomb, memories pressed around her again. Like clothes snatched from a washing-line, she gathered up the images that flapped in front of her and took them for burial, symbolizing her love and the penitence with which her Lord would be enfolded in death, but also the bonds of captivity which he had taken upon himself in his momentous engagement with evil and the forces of destruction.

In fact it was the sight of the empty winding-sheets that startled her most. That which had bound her could not bind him. From the threads of her disordered life and love a new creation had emerged. The restoration of life in the healing moment of her first encounter with Jesus now found affirmation in proclamation and witness; she it was he sent to tell the others; she it was who first communicated with devastating simplicity the news of our reconciliation: 'I have seen the Lord.'

Places and people exercise a great power in our memory. It is often said that one can forgive but never forget. In the great drama of the experience of death and resurrection, which we know in baptism, which we renew each Easter and celebrate each Sunday, our memory of hurts and wrongs is not obliterated. The story of our lives is not rewritten, but is, as it were, rewoven. Every detail is there, it is the shroud of death in which the Lord is bound and laid in the tomb. Only in the glory of the resurrection does it take on new significance, not because it is different, but because he is, and therefore so are we.

Lord God,

you brought us healing through the Easter mysteries.
Continue to be bountiful to your people:
lead us to the perfect freedom,
by which the joy that gladdens our way on earth
will be fulfilled in heaven.
We make our prayer through our Lord. Amen.

Student Cross
musicians

ASCENDED AND GLORIFIED, OUR HIGH PRIEST

Since in Jesus, the Son of God, we have the supreme high priest who has gone through to the highest heaven, we must hold firm to our profession of faith. For the high priest we have is not incapable of feeling our weaknesses with us, but has been put to the test in exactly the same way as ourselves, apart from sin. Let us, then, have no fear in approaching the throne of grace to receive mercy and to find grace when we are in need of help.

HEBREWS 4: 14–16

It was only on Ascension Day that he thought that he might eventually begin to understand. Ever since he had returned from what was still referred to as the 'mission field', his life in general, and his faith in particular, had failed to make sense.

He had spent the last eleven years of his life out there, working in a hospital which served everyone who lived in the town and much of the countryside round about. His medical training had equipped him to deal with a wide range of tropical diseases and the recurrent medical problems which are the product of economic hardship in most of the developing nations of the world. But although he was funded by 51 a Missionary Society, nothing had prepared him for the emotional and spiritual impact of the situation he encountered.

Old age was a rare thing; terminal care was entrusted to underqualified, but all too experienced, nursing staff. The routine cases were always complicated by other factors, such as acute malnutrition and the shortage of essential supplies, which made standard methods of treatment inappropriate. But worse, far worse, than all of this was the work with children. Nothing could be more engaging than the songs, games, and laughter of those who played in the streets and called him 'Charlie Doctor', because it made sense to them to do so. But these, generally, were not the children he saw in the hospital.

There was a daily clinic (even on Sundays) to which women from the outlying villages brought their tragic babies, lovingly carried many miles, but destined, too often, to die within days of arrival. In almost every case, the mother had brought with her another one or two or three children who were also in need of medical care. But her concern was for the one she knew was 'very sick'. And when that child died, she sat and mourned with large round eyes, but shed no tears, for the well within her had long since run dry.

For eleven years he had treated their illnesses and shared their tears. These people had been his family; he had participated in their life and made it his own. And now he experienced a grief deeper than anything he had known in Africa. For here in England he saw the same black faces, heard the same happy laughter from their children in the streets, but saw as well the same fatal division between rich and poor. Racism stared at him with insidious persistence, masked in an infinite variety of semi-respectable guises.

It was the African years that made him notice. And although that experience receded in time, it remained with him in every moment of his present life, calling him to notice again and again the needs and hopes and fears of those who had become, long ago, his own. Anger, hatred, even political action provided no adequate outlet for his feelings. But he began to understand the pattern of the life of Jesus with new clarity. What Jesus had taken to himself in the incarnation and experienced in his life on earth remained with him, glorified and ascended into heaven, for all eternity. This experience is not just a series of memories, but out of those memories it becomes a full-blooded sharing in our life, today and forever, as our brother and our priest.

PRAYER

Almighty God,
fill us with a holy joy,
teach us how to thank you with
*   reverence and love*
on account of the ascension of
*   Christ your Son.*
You have raised us up with
*   him:*
where he, the head, has
*   preceded us in glory,*
there we, the body, are called in
*   hope.*
We make our prayer through
*   our Lord. Amen.*

REMEMBERING THE FUTURE

In the Jewish calendar Pentecost was originally an agricultural pilgrimage festival, the Feast of Weeks. 'Two loaves of bread were made from the season's first wheat, and they were presented as "first fruits"' (E. P. Sanders, *Judaism*). Later the feast became associated with the giving of the Law on Mount Sinai. In our own calendar Pentecost stands at the onset of the summer, a pilgrimage time when people come to Walsingham in huge numbers.

It will happen in the final days
that the mountain of Yahweh's house
will rise higher than the mountains
and tower above the heights.
Then all the nations will stream to it,
many peoples will come to it and say,
'Come, let us go up to the mountain
    of Yahweh,
to the house of the God of Jacob
that he may teach us his ways
so that we may walk in his paths.'
For the Law will issue from Zion
and the word of Yahweh from
    Jerusalem.

ISAIAH 2: 1–4

Jerusalem was the place to be for Pentecost. Teeming with people, it throbbed with the excitement and buzz of any pilgrimage centre. There was something familiar about the group of people which had congregated in the upper room: family and close friends of Jesus. They too were caught up in the pilgrimage atmosphere of the place, but for them the sense of expectation was deeper than any they had ever known.

Together once before at a wedding, the *frisson* of excitement and celebration had culminated in a quite unexpected and remarkable disclosure: the gift of wine. Now they wondered. The signs and the language were all around them. Here in the first fruits were the symbols of the kingdom Jesus had so often spoken about: the sower, mustard seed, wheat and darnel, the fruit of the vine, and a great harvest awaiting its labourers. Surely he would reveal his presence among them through these chosen and sacred gifts. And when the moment fell upon them, words spoken by the Baptist came into their minds: 'he will baptise you with the Holy Spirit and fire. His winnowing-fan is in his hand, he will clear his threshing-floor and gather his wheat into his barn.'

Now Mary understood. She heard in the sound of the violent wind the voice which spoke from Sinai, when the old Covenant was given on the mountain and sealed in blood. She saw the tongues of flame and remembered the pillar of cloud and fire which had led a pilgrim people through the wilderness. She listened to the apostles speak and believed that the prophets Joel and Ezekiel, Isaiah, Micah, and Malachi had been vindicated.

Mary saw the outpouring of the Spirit of the Lord and knew that what she remembered was not, in fact, the past, but the future. It had been that way when the Spirit had erupted through her in the outpouring of her joy with Elizabeth. Then, as now, the words which broke forth wove together the threads of the past to display the radiance of the glory of the future. 'When the Spirit of truth comes . . . he will reveal to you the things to come.' Mary understood. She had already, long ago, been overshadowed by the power of the Most High.

The Anglican National Pilgrimage

PRAYER

Lord God,
you sanctify your Church in
*   every race and nation*
by the mystery of Pentecost.
Pour out the gifts of the Holy
*   Spirit on all humanity,*
and fulfil now in the hearts of
*   your faithful*
what you accomplished
when the gospel was first
*   preached on earth.*
We make our prayer through
*   our Lord. Amen.*

GIVEN A SHARE IN
THE RESURRECTION

Basking in the warmth of high summer, the Assumption brings to Walsingham a time of ease and gracious celebration. In many houses along the High Street a statue of Our Lady is placed in the window, attended by flowers and a votive candle. Bunting flutters from pilgrims' hostels, and the streets are paved with the expectation of carnival and festivity.

It isn't all froth, however. Large numbers gather for the Assumptiontide lecture, a recognition that the mind must also be engaged in this celebration which demands the response of a faith in search of understanding. Anglican, Roman Catholic, Free Church, and Orthodox Christians unite to learn from each other the steps which lead on a pilgrimage of truth to the dazzling brightness of the vision of God, in which the senses are numb and all language and reason is like chaff before the wind.

In this school of the Lord's household we learn that the mind must descend into the heart, and the outward expression of our enquiry is to be found, among other places, in liturgical celebration. On the eve of the Assumption there is a procession, a mighty act of witness, and the dramatic presentation of our Christian destiny.

Late in the evening people of all Christian traditions and none gather with lighted candles in the Anglican parish church. They read from the scriptures and meditate upon the joyful event which marks the dawn of our salvation: the birth of Jesus. Slowly the procession makes its way up into Friday Market to the Roman Catholic parish church. Gathered around the cross the pilgrims hear, through the Word of God and in prayer, the events of the Lord's passion and death, the mystery of our redemption. By now it is dark, and cautiously the procession embarks upon the final stage of its journey.

In the gardens of the Anglican Shrine the image of Mary is placed beneath the dome of the Hickleton Altar, surrounded by a blaze of votive candles. Scripture readings, prayers, and hymns surge through the pilgrim gathering to celebrate our glory and our hope: the triumph of the resurrection, the joy of the ascension, and the renewing, liberating power of the gift of the Holy Spirit. Mary is the sign of the outcome of this hope. The wonders of God which she recalled from the past have now been realized in her future as she shares in the resurrection: 'the Almighty has done great things for me. Holy is his name.'

In the exuberance of this great rejoicing, rockets soar into the night sky and cascade in showers of starlets and gleaming lights. The journey into darkness has issued in an outpouring of heaven-like light, a symbol of the Christian way. To give expression to this hope, the scriptures place together the elements of creation as crown, throne, and diadem for a woman whose act of giving birth enables us to hope for a place in the new heaven and the new earth. Destined for this, we have already dimly glimpsed her, 'robed with the sun, standing on the moon, and on her head a crown of twelve stars.'

In my estimation, all that we suffer in the present time is nothing in comparison with the glory which is destined to be disclosed for us, for the whole creation is waiting with eagerness for the children of God to be revealed . . . We are well aware that the whole creation, until this time, has been groaning in labour pains. And not only that: we too, who have the first-fruits of the Spirit, even we are groaning inside ourselves, waiting with eagerness for our bodies to be set free.

ROMANS 8: 18–19, 22–3

Celebrating the Assumption

PRAYER

*Almighty Father of our Lord
Jesus Christ,
you have revealed the beauty
of your power
by exalting the lowly virgin of
Nazareth
and making her the mother of
our Saviour.
May the prayers of this woman
clothed with the sun
bring Jesus to the waiting
world
and fill the void of
incompletion
with the presence of her child
who lives and reigns for ever
and ever. Amen.*

Our Lady of Walsingham

BLESSED ARE YOU

At this time the disciples came to Jesus and said, 'Who is the greatest in the kingdom of Heaven?' So he called a little child to him whom he set among them. Then he said, 'In truth I tell you, unless you change and become like little children you will never enter the kingdom of Heaven. And so, the one who makes himself as little as this little child is the greatest in the kingdom of Heaven. Anyone who welcomes one little child like this in my name welcomes me.'

MATTHEW 18: 1–5

There is nothing more poignant, more utterly sad or overwhelmingly inexplicable, than the death of a child. Endless questions flood the mind: how could a loving God permit such a thing? Does time heal the grief? And everlastingly, why?

The Anglican National Pilgrimage

Jesus points us very clearly to the way in which children can exemplify the qualities required for becoming a citizen of heaven. From the rest of the gospel evidence we get an impression of what these qualities might be. Children are vulnerable (Matthew 17: 14–20); they inspire great faith in those who care for them (Matthew 8: 5–13); they are capable of simple generosity (John 6: 5–15); they invite others to share their dances and their songs (Matthew 11: 16–19).

In order to enter the world of children it is necessary to understand and demonstrate such qualities. With them we cannot be defensive; they ask us to be gentle. They want to know what we believe in, and why, and how much it means to us; they ask us to hunger and thirst for uprightness. They do not respect meanness; they ask us to be merciful. They are unimpressed by the dignity of those who choose not to stoop to share their stories and their games; they ask us to be the poor in spirit. This is the world of those who reflect the qualities of the beatitudes, the world of Mary, the most blessed of all women.

But Mary also knows how easily this world of gospel values is overturned

The National Ecumenical Youth Pilgrimage

by other forces, more persuasive, more destructive, and more transient. She encountered them in the crowd which bayed for the blood of her Son and then laid his broken body in her arms. And she remembers them in the cries of the mothers of Bethlehem who howled with inconsolable grief at the death of their little children, the moment when the death warrant of her own child was first signed.

Out of these terrible deaths comes blessedness, the blessedness of every innocent victim and of those who mourn, a blessedness which finds its home in the kingdom of heaven. Gathered there are the children, young and old, who revealed the qualities of this kingdom here on earth. And there a place is also found for the patriarchs and prophets, the Apostles and martyrs, missionaries, pastors, holy men and holy women whose saintly lives were seen by God but unrecorded by the world. With this innumerable and royal throng Mary shares a place; upon her is laid the title 'Queen' and a coronet, from which there is reflected the glory of the saints, bathed in the refulgent splendour of the throne of God and of the Lamb.

READING AND PRAYER

After that I saw that there was a huge number, impossible
for anyone to count, of people from every nation, race,
tribe and language; they were standing in front of the
throne and in front of the Lamb, dressed in white robes
and holding palms in their hands. They shouted in a loud
voice, 'Salvation to our God, who sits on the throne, and
to the Lamb!' And all the angels who were standing in a
circle round the throne, surrounding the elders and the
four living creatures, prostrated themselves before the
throne, and touched the ground with their foreheads,
worshipping God with these words:

> Amen. Praise and glory and wisdom,
> thanksgiving and honour and power and strength
> to our God for ever and ever. Amen.

REVELATION 7: 9–12

AUTUMN

Baptismal Mysteries

THE BAPTISM OF THE LORD

Autumn leaves are a gardener's nightmare. No sooner have the lawns been cleared than a fresh lot has fallen. But nothing can compare with the haunting smell they produce on the bonfire, the thin wisps of smoke evocative of many things. For the poet Virgil these leaves brought to mind the image of the dead who have descended to the underworld, 'Multitudinous as the leaves that fall in a forest at the first frost of autumn.'

Autumn covers much of that span of the Church's year in which we reflect upon the mystery of how the events of the Lord's birth and life, death and resurrection, must, through baptism, shape our own lives. It is a time for remembrance, culminating in the great season of Advent, the coming of the Lord in judgement, when all that we are and have been will be revealed. And though the falling leaves remind us of the finite nature of our existence, yet in the beauty of their russet shades they evoke as well a glory which is still incomplete in the way of God's revealing.

He came to Nazara, where he had been brought up, and went into the synagogue on the Sabbath day as he usually did. He stood up to read, and they handed him the scroll of the prophet Isaiah. Unrolling the scroll he found the place where it is written:

> *The spirit of the Lord is on me,*
> *for he has anointed me*
> *to bring the good news to the afflicted.*
> *He has sent me to proclaim liberty to captives,*
> *sight to the blind,*
> *to let the oppressed go free,*
> *to proclaim a year of favour from the Lord.*

He then rolled up the scroll, gave it back to the assistant and sat down. And all eyes in the synagogue were fixed on him. Then he began to speak to them, 'This text is being fulfilled today even while you are listening.' And he won the approval of all, and they were astonished by the gracious words that came from his lips.

70   LUKE 4: 16–22

At his baptism in the river Jordan, that spirit of which Jesus spoke had been seen to descend upon him, awakening faith and acclaiming him as the beloved of the Father. It was a decisive moment, revealing an identity which was always his, and displaying to the world the purposes of God. Now, at the beginning of his public ministry among the people of Galilee, Jesus outlines his agenda, extending this work of revelation to embrace their hopes and desires, of which he is the fulfilment.

Jesus' experience of baptism is also ours; it awakens faith and reveals to us our true identity. We recognize our finitude but also the veins of grace which give colour and beauty to our lives. Unlike the passive leaves in Virgil's poem however, grace in us is dynamic and creative. It draws us into relationships with others and our Creator in a magnificent collage of substance, colour, and shape. And through the interaction, blending, and fusion of our colours, the divine majesty of God painstakingly reworks us into the order of his spectrum which is the rainbow harmony of the covenant he has made with all creation.

The Seven Sacrament Font in St Mary's

PRAYER

Almighty, eternal God,
when the Spirit descended
*   upon Jesus*
at his baptism in the Jordan,
you revealed him as your own
*   beloved Son.*
Keep us, your children born of
*   water and the Spirit,*
faithful to our calling.
We ask this in the name of
*   Jesus the Lord. Amen.*

INSTRUCTION ON PRAYER

It was watching him, silent and alone, that made the disciples ask for instruction on prayer.

'Ask, and it will be given to you; search, and you will find; knock, and the door will be opened to you. Everyone who asks receives; everyone who searches finds; everyone who knocks will have the door opened. Is there anyone among you who would hand his son a stone when he asked for bread? Or would hand him a snake when he asked for a fish? If you, then, evil as you are, know how to give your children what is good, how much more will your Father in heaven give good things to those who ask him!'

MATTHEW 7: 7–11

There are relatively few places in the gospels which speak of Jesus praying. But the moment when his prayer is described most vividly is in the garden of Gethsemane. The prayer begun at that moment is continued into the prison cell, the judgement hall, and along every step of the way to Calvary. It resounds in his mind during the excruciating hours of his agony on the cross, and culminates in the moment when the door of death is opened to him and he gains access to those whose misery and longing haunted every part of his ministry in Galilee.

In the sense of being an overpowering emotion, the word 'passion' would do well as a description of prayer. The words used by Jesus in his instruction on prayer have a cumulative effect which suggests just this element of vehemence. The way of prayer which he describes is the active engagement of someone totally absorbed in a particular quest. Ask, search, and knock, and elsewhere he suggests, go on knocking, batter the door, bring to God all that is in your heart.

This passionate prayer is something which Jesus encounters again and again. It assails him accusingly in the twisted face of the man possessed in the synagogue at Capernaum. It clamours from the sceptical crowd, as the man whose hand was withered stands silently before him one Sabbath day. It touches him unmistakably in the press of a throng which hides within it a woman, desperate and believing. It echoes from the rocks and tombs which are the home of Legion, cries out from lepers and the blind, and is written on the face of every parent whose child is close to death.

As Jesus enters into passionate prayer in Gethsemane, do not these images haunt his memory, for they are the reason he is there? It was for them that he healed on the Sabbath, for them he ate and drank with sinners and outcasts, for them he forgave sins, which, as God, only he could do. Now, and for all eternity, Jesus prays passionately, receiving every action of prayer which asks, searches, and knocks at the gate of heaven.

And today, his mind is haunted by every pilgrim who lights a candle or descends the steps of the holy well to be sprinkled, who hesitantly scratches down an intercession, or sits to whisper the name of a friend in trouble. With infinite care, he listens to the lists of those who keep their asking in well-ordered form, and he receives with searing compassion the handicapped, tortured, and disordered spirits who recognize him in their cries, which were first declared protestingly in a Galilean synagogue on the Sabbath day. In every action of asking, seeking, and knocking in prayer, the beloved Son hears re-echo from the world the words he taught, 'Our Father', and knows that there are hearts that long to see his will done on earth as it is in heaven.

PRAYER

Our Father in heaven,
may your name be held holy,
your kingdom come,
your will be done,
on earth as in heaven.

Give us today our daily bread.
And forgive us our debts,
as we have forgiven those who are in debt to us.
And do not put us to the test,
but save us from the Evil One. Amen.

New Dawn
Pilgrimage

RESTORING THE AFFLICTED

And going into Peter's house Jesus found Peter's mother-in-law in bed and feverish. He touched her hand and the fever left her, and she got up and began to serve him. That evening they brought him many who were possessed by devils. He drove out the spirits with a command and cured all who were sick. This was to fulfil what was spoken by the prophet Isaiah:

> 'He himself bore our sicknesses away and carried our diseases.'

MATTHEW 8: 14–17

It was late autumn when she came alone to make a pilgrimage in search of healing, healing of the memory and the recovery of her life. The bare trees stood stark against a leaden sky and cold northern winds heralded the onset of winter.

Little less than a year ago Lysoma had been the contented mother of five children, and she was comforted for the death of her husband by the reflection of him in each of them. Her son Nkiku had insisted on returning to the country of his birth, to contribute what he could to its economic development and stabilization.

The phone call which brought to England news of his murder rang with an inevitability which Lysoma had always feared. The motive was the theft of less than £20; the effect on her was devastating. She flew out to bury him among the people whose life he had wanted to share. She returned, desolate and empty, and on a cold November day sat in the Chapel of Reconciliation, wondering how to go on living.

She had asked before arriving in Walsingham to speak with Sister Gabriel, one of the sisters who was then working at the Shrine. This was the cry from one woman to another for help, for the sharing of tears, and discernment of the way ahead. Sister Gabriel spoke to her of Mary the mother of Jesus as a guide for the bereaved and the sorrowing. Together the women set out to make the Stations of the Cross. At each bleak wooden cross they stopped and exchanged their memories; Lysoma told the newer story of a flight to Africa and her journey to the scene of the murder investigation; from Mary's life Sister Gabriel narrated a more familiar sequence of events.

Jesus is made to carry his cross. 'Nkiku was threatened; they wanted money, but he had none with him, he knew the dangers.' He falls for the first time. 'They'd been watching his flat because they knew that he travelled abroad and he often had foreign currency.' Simon of Cyrene helps Jesus to carry the cross. 'We couldn't understand why no one saw anything; we think they were afraid to speak.' Jesus dies on the cross. 'There were three gunshot wounds.' And the body of Jesus was laid in the tomb.

The
Pilgrimage
of the Sick

For a long time Lysoma stood by the fourteenth station, staring at the ground and remembering the day when she too had buried her son. Very gently Sister Gabriel took her by the arm and led her to another station. There they heard a different message: 'There is no need for you to be afraid. I know you are looking for Jesus, who was crucified. He is not here, for he has risen, as he said he would.'

Mary's shared experience as a grieving mother led Lysoma along the path to where she could encounter Jesus newly risen from the dead. In that encounter Lysoma recognized the Lord who embraces all women and men in death and offers the possibility of new life in his resurrection. His ransom from death became her liberation from despair, and by his stripes she was healed.

PRAYER

God of unchanging power and
*   light,*
look with mercy and favour on
*   your entire Church.*
Bring lasting salvation to all
*   humanity,*
so that the world may see
the fallen lifted up,
the old made new,
and all things brought to
*   perfection,*
through him who is their
*   origin,*
our Lord Jesus Christ,
who lives and reigns for ever
*   and ever. Amen.*

THE FEEDING OF THE FIVE THOUSAND

All is now quiet in the village. The routine of an agricultural community reasserts itself as the only interruption to the stillness of this fold in the hills which marks a turn in the Stiffkey valley. But pilgrims have left behind the signs of their presence.

Signalling new contours imposed on village life, a signpost points to the coach park, marking out the authorized route. The silent road is rutted and muddy. Displaced gravel and the occasional pothole bear witness to the heavy imprint of wheels which have carried pilgrims from Morecambe and

Tyneside, from the Potteries and the South of Wales, from London, Brighton, and the south coast stretching down to Plymouth and Penzance.

The holy mile, along which pilgrims in their thousands walk each year, seems to be deserted and silent except for the hooting of the pheasants, and if it is Monday, there is shooting in the woods up at Snoring. A solitary figure walks the dog in the direction of Houghton St Giles. From the wooded hedgerow and at each bend and junction, the final echo of a pilgrim 'ave' is now almost inaudible.

Turning to the Abbey grounds, the Priory arch gathers around itself an area of grassy terrace, and points to the grandeur of human folly and decay, though whispering, too, a message of the higher grandeur of the ways of God, who from the broken fragments of our history's sad divisions works new ways to draw us to himself. The gardens here stretch out, a green table on which, in the eucharist, the bread of heaven has been generously supplied to pilgrim crowds.

The remembrance of these gatherings sweeps us in procession to the forecourt of the Anglican Shrine. In this sanctuary of the Holy House a sign is given that the Lord in glory lives among us. The image of Our Lady and her child reveals the truth to which an eastern poet gives testimony with incomparable grace:

Once more they ventured from the dust to raise
Their eyes—up to the Throne—into the blaze,
And in the centre of the glory there
Behold the figure of—**themselves**—as 'twere
Transfigured—looking to themselves, beheld
The figure on the Throne en-miracled,
Until their eyes themselves and **that** between
Did hesitate which **Seer** was, which **Seen**.

For we become that child when he becomes our flesh and blood in gifts of bread and wine, and in communion feeds us with himself. Here the bread that comes down from heaven is kept and given to the thousands who have passed this way on pilgrimage. Though faint whispers of their presence tell us that as human beings we are transient, frail, dust, and that echoes of our lives will one day fade away, yet none the less the bread which Jesus offers pilgrims year by year is heavenly food, and gives to all who taste a share in his immortal life.

He gave orders that the people were to sit down on the grass; then he took the five loaves and the two fish, raised his eyes to heaven and said the blessing. And breaking the loaves he handed them to his disciples, who gave them to the crowds. They all ate as much as they wanted, and they collected the scraps left over, twelve baskets full.

MATTHEW 14: 19–21

PRAYER

Lord our God,
in this great sacrament
we come into the presence of
*   Jesus Christ, your Son,*
born of the Virgin Mary
and crucified for our salvation.
May we who declare our faith
*   in this fountain of love and*
*   mercy*
drink from it the water of
*   everlasting life.*
We ask this in the name of
*   Jesus, the Lord. Amen.*

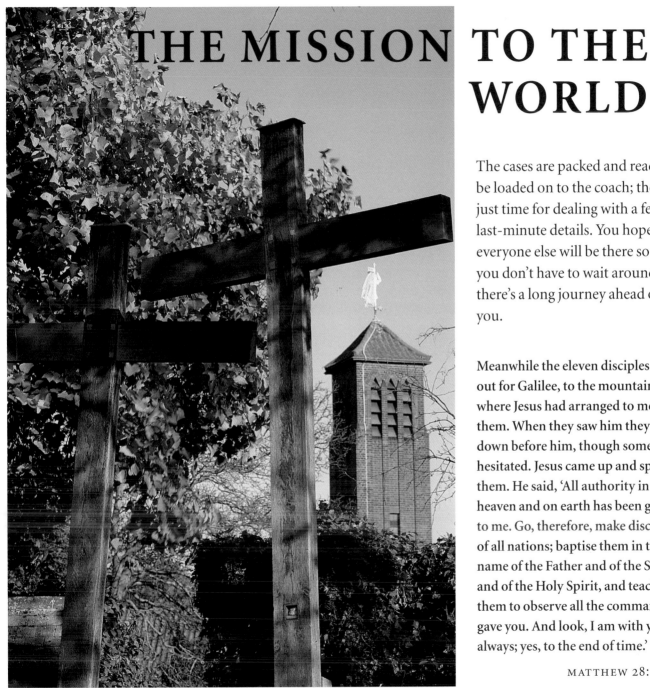

THE MISSION TO THE WORLD

The cases are packed and ready to be loaded on to the coach; there's just time for dealing with a few last-minute details. You hope everyone else will be there so that you don't have to wait around; there's a long journey ahead of you.

Meanwhile the eleven disciples set out for Galilee, to the mountain where Jesus had arranged to meet them. When they saw him they fell down before him, though some hesitated. Jesus came up and spoke to them. He said, 'All authority in heaven and on earth has been given to me. Go, therefore, make disciples of all nations; baptise them in the name of the Father and of the Son and of the Holy Spirit, and teach them to observe all the commands I gave you. And look, I am with you always; yes, to the end of time.'

MATTHEW 28: 16–20   85

As for the disciples, so for us; the journey home is filled with strange but wonderful impressions. Perhaps new friendships have been made, or old quarrels forgiven. There might be one particular moment which was special: a candle lit for someone you love; the singing of a favourite hymn, or the learning of a new one; receiving the laying on of hands for the first time; being asked to read at Mass. Sometimes there is an almost tangible awareness of having been given admittance to the company of the angels and the saints. It is like an icon which you want to take home and show to others. But in this case, you have to try to put it into words, and rarely can the depth and magnificence of the experience be captured in its entirety.

It is often tempting to stay. Pilgrims speak wistfully of the wonderful atmosphere of peace in Walsingham, and reflect

on how lovely it must be to live there. But in fact we come, like the shepherds and the Magi, to bring gifts; the gifts of our prayers, our adoration, our thanksgiving, ourselves. And such is the nature of God that he always gives us far more in return; he gives us himself. So when this awesome exchange of gifts is completed, we must, following others who have travelled to the house of the Holy Family, return to our own homes, transformed by what we have seen, heard, and done.

The journey home is equally a pilgrimage, though to a different kind of holy place. For it is in our homes and among the people with whom we share our lives, that we are called to reveal and proclaim the presence of God and the glory of his saints and angels. In a holy place like Walsingham, whatever we experience issues in the renewal of baptismal grace. And the Lord himself then says: 'Go, make disciples, teach them my commands, and look, I am with you.'

So the coaches, cars, and minibuses make the pilgrimage home, to travel north through Newark, journey west through Wisbech, or turn south to Swaffham, Brandon, and the A11. As you go, remember Mary, returning through the hill country of Judah from her visit to Elizabeth to proclaim the song which has echoed from the lips of Christians in every generation who have called her blessed. Recall her journey home from Egypt and, after the visit twelve years later back to Jerusalem, a journey back to Nazareth with Joseph and her son, to home and familiar streets, to work and school, to neighbours, and the things that get you down. In this memory rejoice, since it is at home that you are called to be like Jesus and to increase in wisdom, in stature, and in favour with people and with God.

PRAYER

Father in heaven,
form in us the likeness of your Son
and deepen his life within us.
Send us as witnesses of gospel joy
into a world of fragile peace and broken promises.
Touch the hearts of all people with your love
that they in turn may love one another.
We ask this in the name of Jesus, the Lord.
Amen.